What Cats Teach Us®

LIFE'S LESSONS LEARNED FROM OUR FELINE FRIENDS · 18-MONTH CALENDAR · 2020

A smile makes everyone feel better.

WILLOW CREEK

August 2019

SUN	MON	TUE	WED	THU	FRI	SAT
				1	2	3
4	5	6	7	8	9	10
11	12	13	14	15	16	17
18	19	20	21	22	23	24
25	26	27	28	29	30	31

July 2019

SUN	MON	TUE	WED	THU	FRI	SAT
	1	2	3	4	5	6
7	8	9	10	11	12	13
14	15	16	17	18	19	20
21	22	23	24	25	26	27
28	29	30	31			

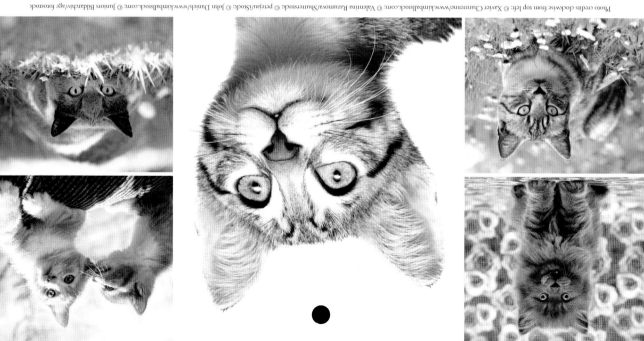

September 2019

SUN	MON	TUE	WED	THU	FRI	SAT
1	2	3	4	5	6	7
8	9	10	11	12	13	14
15	16	17	18	19	20	21
22	23	24	25	26	27	28
29	30					

October 2019

SUN	MON	TUE	WED	THU	FRI	SAT
		1	2	3	4	5
6	7	8	9	10	11	12
13	14	15	16	17	18	19
20	21	22	23	24	25	26
27	28	29	30	31		

November 2019

SUN	MON	TUE	WED	THU	FRI	SAT
					1	2
3	4	5	6	7	8	9
10	11	12	13	14	15	16
17	18	19	20	21	22	23
24	25	26	27	28	29	30

December 2019

SUN	MON	TUE	WED	THU	FRI	SAT
1	2	3	4	5	6	7
8	9	10	11	12	13	14
15	16	17	18	19	20	21
22	23	24	25	26	27	28
29	30	31				

Toll Free 1-800-850-9453
www.WillowCreekPress.com

JANUARY

A smile makes everyone feel better.

SUNDAY	MONDAY	TUESDAY	WEDNESDAY	THURSDAY	FRIDAY	SATURDAY
December 2019 S M T W T F S 1 2 3 4 5 6 7 8 9 10 11 12 13 14 15 16 17 18 19 20 21 22 23 24 25 26 27 28 29 30 31 1 2 3 4	February 2020 S M T W T F S 26 27 28 29 30 31 1 2 3 4 5 6 7 8 9 10 11 12 13 14 15 16 17 18 19 20 21 22 23 24 25 26 27 28 29	31	1 New Year's Day	2　First Quarter ◗	3	4
5	6 Epiphany	7	8	9	10　Full Moon ○	11
12	13	14	15	16	17　Last Quarter ◗	18
19	20 Martin Luther King, Jr. Day	21	22	23	24　New Moon ●	25 Lunar New Year (Year of the Rat)
26	27 Australia Day Observed (AUS)	28	29	30	31	1

© Valentina Razumova/Shutterstock

FEBRUARY

Be proud of your abilities.

SUNDAY	MONDAY	TUESDAY	WEDNESDAY	THURSDAY	FRIDAY	SATURDAY
January 2020 S M T W T F S 29 30 31 1 2 3 4 5 6 7 8 9 10 11 12 13 14 15 16 17 18 19 20 21 22 23 24 25 26 27 28 29 30 31 1	**March 2020** S M T W T F S 1 2 3 4 5 6 7 8 9 10 11 12 13 14 15 16 17 18 19 20 21 22 23 24 25 26 27 28 29 30 31 1 2 3 4	28	29	30	31	1 First Quarter ◑
2 Groundhog Day	3	4	5	6 Waitangi Day (NZ)	7	8
9 Full Moon ○	10	11	12 Lincoln's Birthday	13	14 Valentine's Day	15 Last Quarter ◑
16	17 President's Day Family Day (CAN-AB, BC, NB, ON, SK) Heritage Day (CAN-NS)	18	19	20	21	22 Washington's Birthday
23 New Moon ●	24	25 Fat Tuesday (Mardi Gras)	26 Ash Wednesday	27	28	29

MARCH

SUNDAY	MONDAY	TUESDAY	WEDNESDAY	THURSDAY	FRIDAY	SATURDAY
1	2 First Quarter ◑	3	4	5	6	7
8 Daylight Saving Time Begins	9 Full Moon ○ Commonwealth Day (CAN, UK, AUS)	10 Purim	11	12	13	14
15	16 Last Quarter ◐	17 St. Patrick's Day	18	19 Spring Equinox	20	21
22 Mothering Sunday (UK)	23	24 New Moon ●	25	26	27	28
29	30	31	1	2		

February 2020

S	M	T	W	T	F	S
26	27	28	29	30	31	1
2	3	4	5	6	7	8
9	10	11	12	13	14	15
16	17	18	19	20	21	22
23	24	25	26	27	28	29

April 2020

S	M	T	W	T	F	S
29	30	31	1	2	3	4
5	6	7	8	9	10	11
12	13	14	15	16	17	18
19	20	21	22	23	24	25
26	27	28	29	30	1	2

APRIL

Live life to the fullest.

SUNDAY	MONDAY	TUESDAY	WEDNESDAY	THURSDAY	FRIDAY	SATURDAY

March 2020

S	M	T	W	T	F	S
1	2	3	4	5	6	7
8	9	10	11	12	13	14
15	16	17	18	19	20	21
22	23	24	25	26	27	28
29	30	31	1	2	3	4

May 2020

S	M	T	W	T	F	S
26	27	28	29	30	1	2
3	4	5	6	7	8	9
10	11	12	13	14	15	16
17	18	19	20	21	22	23
24	25	26	27	28	29	30
31	1	2	3	4	5	6

31

1 First Quarter
April Fool's Day

2

3

4

5
Palm Sunday

6

7 Full Moon

8
Passover Begins

9

10
Good Friday

11

12
Easter Sunday

13
Easter Monday

14 Last Quarter

15
Income Tax Deadline

16
Passover Ends
Emancipation Day

17

18

19
Greek Orthodox Easter

20

21

22 New Moon
Earth Day
Admin. Professionals Day

23
Ramadan Begins
St. George's Day (UK)

24
Arbor Day

25

26

27
Anzac Day (NZ, AUS)

28

29

30 First Quarter

1

2

© Eric Isselée/Shutterstock

MAY

Fresh air will lift your spirits.

SUNDAY	MONDAY	TUESDAY	WEDNESDAY	THURSDAY	FRIDAY	SATURDAY
April 2020 / June 2020		28	29	30	1 — Labor Day (MX)	2
3	4 — Early May Bank Holiday (UK, IRL)	5 — Cinco de Mayo (MX)	6	7 — Full Moon ○ — National Day of Prayer	8	9
10 — Mother's Day	11	12	13	14 — Last Quarter ◗	15	16 — Armed Forces Day
17	18 — Victoria Day (CAN)	19	20	21	22 — New Moon ●	23 — Ramadan Ends
24 — Eid al-Fitr / 31 — Pentecost	25 — Memorial Day / Spring Bank Holiday (UK)	26	27	28	29 — First Quarter ◗	30

April 2020

S M T W T F S
29 30 31 1 2 3 4
5 6 7 8 9 10 11
12 13 14 15 16 17 18
19 20 21 22 23 24 25
26 27 28 29 30 1 2

June 2020

S M T W T F S
31 1 2 3 4 5 6
7 8 9 10 11 12 13
14 15 16 17 18 19 20
21 22 23 24 25 26 27
28 29 30 1 2 3 4

JUNE

Go ahead and flaunt your style.

SUNDAY	MONDAY	TUESDAY	WEDNESDAY	THURSDAY	FRIDAY	SATURDAY
31	1	2	3	4	5 Full Moon ○	6
	Queen's Birthday (NZ)					D-Day
7	8	9	10	11	12	13 Last Quarter ◑
	Queen's Birthday (AUS)					
14	15	16	17	18	19	20
Flag Day						Summer Solstice
21 New Moon ●	22	23	24	25	26	27
Father's Day			St. Jean-Baptiste Day (Quebec)			
28 First Quarter ◐	29	30	1	2		

May 2020							July 2020						
S	M	T	W	T	F	S	S	M	T	W	T	F	S
26	27	28	29	30	1	2	28	29	30	1	2	3	4
3	4	5	6	7	8	9	5	6	7	8	9	10	11
10	11	12	13	14	15	16	12	13	14	15	16	17	18
17	18	19	20	21	22	23	19	20	21	22	23	24	25
24	25	26	27	28	29	30	26	27	28	29	30	31	1
31	1	2	3	4	5	6							

JULY

Don't let obstacles get in your way.

SUNDAY	MONDAY	TUESDAY	WEDNESDAY	THURSDAY	FRIDAY	SATURDAY
June 2020 S M T W T F S 31 1 2 3 4 5 6 7 8 9 10 11 12 13 14 15 16 17 18 19 20 21 22 23 24 25 26 27 28 29 30 1 2 3 4	August 2020 S M T W T F S 26 27 28 29 30 31 1 2 3 4 5 6 7 8 9 10 11 12 13 14 15 16 17 18 19 20 21 22 23 24 25 26 27 28 29 30 31 1 2 3 4 5	30	1 Canada Day	2	3	4 Full Moon ○ Independence Day
5	6	7	8	9	10	11
12 Last Quarter ◑ Battle of the Boyne (N. IRL)	13	14 Bastille Day (FRA)	15	16	17	18
19	20 New Moon ●	21	22	23	24	25
26	27 First Quarter ◑	28	29	30	31	1

AUGUST

Play more; worry less.

SUNDAY	MONDAY	TUESDAY	WEDNESDAY	THURSDAY	FRIDAY	SATURDAY
July 2020 S M T W T F S 28 29 30 1 2 3 4 5 6 7 8 9 10 11 12 13 14 15 16 17 18 19 20 21 22 23 24 25 26 27 28 29 30 31 1	**September 2020** S M T W T F S 30 31 1 2 3 4 5 6 7 8 9 10 11 12 13 14 15 16 17 18 19 20 21 22 23 24 25 26 27 28 29 30 1 2 3	28	29	30	31	1
2	3 Full Moon ○ Civic Holiday (CAN) Heritage Day (CAN-AB)	4	5	6	7	8
9	10	11 Last Quarter ◑	12	13	14	15 Assumption of the Blessed Virgin Mary
16	17	18 New Moon ●	19	20	21	22
23	24	25 First Quarter ◑	26	27	28	29
30	31 Summer Bank Holiday (UK)					

© Juniors Bildarchiv/age fotostock

SEPTEMBER

Make happiness a priority.

SUNDAY	MONDAY	TUESDAY	WEDNESDAY	THURSDAY	FRIDAY	SATURDAY
30	31	1	2 Full Moon ○	3	4	5
6	7	8	9	10 Last Quarter ◐	11	12
Father's Day (AUS)	Labor Day				Patriot Day	
13	14	15	16	17 New Moon ●	18	19
Grandparent's Day			Independence Day (MX)		Rosh Hashanah Begins	
20	21	22	23 First Quarter ◑	24	25	26
Rosh Hashanah Ends	UN International Day of Peace	Fall Equinox				
27	28	29	30	1		
Yom Kippur Begins	Queen's Birthday (W. AUS) Yom Kippur Ends					

August 2020						
S	M	T	W	T	F	S
26	27	28	29	30	31	1
2	3	4	5	6	7	8
9	10	11	12	13	14	15
16	17	18	19	20	21	22
23	24	25	26	27	28	29
30	31	1	2	3	4	5

October 2020						
S	M	T	W	T	F	S
27	28	29	30	1	2	3
4	5	6	7	8	9	10
11	12	13	14	15	16	17
18	19	20	21	22	23	24
25	26	27	28	29	30	31

OCTOBER

The chase is better than the catch.

SUNDAY	MONDAY	TUESDAY	WEDNESDAY	THURSDAY	FRIDAY	SATURDAY
September 2020 S M T W T F S 30 31 1 2 3 4 5 6 7 8 9 10 11 12 13 14 15 16 17 18 19 20 21 22 23 24 25 26 27 28 29 30 1 2 3	November 2020 S M T W T F S 1 2 3 4 5 6 7 8 9 10 11 12 13 14 15 16 17 18 19 20 21 22 23 24 25 26 27 28 29 30 1 2 3 4 5	29	30	1 Full Moon ○	2 Sukkot Begins	3
4	5	6	7	8	9 Last Quarter ◖ Sukkot Ends	10
11	12 Columbus Day Thanksgiving Day (CAN)	13	14	15	16 New Moon ● Boss's Day	17 Sweetest Day
18	19	20	21	22	23 First Quarter ◗	24 United Nations Day
25	26 Labour Day (NZ)	27	28	29	30	31 Full Moon ○ Halloween

© John Daniels/www.kimballstock.com

NOVEMBER

Embrace change.

SUNDAY	MONDAY	TUESDAY	WEDNESDAY	THURSDAY	FRIDAY	SATURDAY
1 Daylight Saving Time Ends All Saints Day	2 All Souls Day (Dia de los Muertos)	3 Election Day	4	5 Guy Fawkes Day (UK)	6	7
8 Last Quarter ◖ Remembrance Sunday (UK)	9	10	11 Veteran's Day Remembrance Day (CAN)	12	13	14 New Moon ● Diwali
15	16	17	18	19	20 Mexican Revolution Day	21 First Quarter ◗
22	23	24	25	26 Thanksgiving Day	27	28
29	30 Full Moon ○	1	2	3		

October 2020						
S	M	T	W	T	F	S
27	28	29	30	1	2	3
4	5	6	7	8	9	10
11	12	13	14	15	16	17
18	19	20	21	22	23	24
25	26	27	28	29	30	31

December 2020						
S	M	T	W	T	F	S
29	30	1	2	3	4	5
6	7	8	9	10	11	12
13	14	15	16	17	18	19
20	21	22	23	24	25	26
27	28	29	30	31	1	2

DECEMBER

SUNDAY	MONDAY	TUESDAY	WEDNESDAY	THURSDAY	FRIDAY	SATURDAY
29	30	1	2	3	4	5
6	7 Last Quarter ◐	8	9	10	11	12
	Pearl Harbor Remembrance Day			Hanukkah Begins		Fiesta of Our Lady of Guadalupe (MX)
13	14 New Moon ●	15	16	17	18	19
					Hanukkah Ends	
20	21 First Quarter ◑	22	23	24	25	26
	Winter Solstice			Christmas Eve	Christmas Day	Kwanzaa (until Jan. 1st) Boxing Day (CAN, UK)
27	28	29 Full Moon ○	30	31		
				New Year's Eve		

November 2020

S	M	T	W	T	F	S
1	2	3	4	5	6	7
8	9	10	11	12	13	14
15	16	17	18	19	20	21
22	23	24	25	26	27	28
29	30	1	2	3	4	5

January 2021

S	M	T	W	T	F	S
27	28	29	30	31	1	2
3	4	5	6	7	8	9
10	11	12	13	14	15	16
17	18	19	20	21	22	23
24	25	26	27	28	29	30
31	1	2	3	4	5	6

A smile makes everyone feel better.

Be proud of your abilities.

Try to live in harmony with one another.

Live life to the fullest.

Fresh air will lift your spirits.

Go ahead and flaunt your style.

Don't let obstacles get in your way.

Play more; worry less.

Make happiness a priority.

The chase is better than the catch.

Embrace change.

What Cats Teach Us®

LIFE'S LESSONS LEARNED FROM OUR FELINE FRIENDS • 2020

• 18-month calendar featuring six bonus months
of July through December of 2019.
• Large boxes to record dates and special events.
• Includes moon phases, U.S. and international holidays.

■ WILLOW CREEK PRESS®

USA $7.99
CAN $9.99 / AU RRP $10.00
NZ RRP $12.99 / UK £5.99

ISBN: 978-1-5492-0864-5

DECEMBER						
25	30	31	1	2	3	4
6	7	8	9	10	11	12
13	14	15	16	17	18	19
20	21	22	23	24	25	26
27	28	29	30	31		